FRACTIONS, DECIMALS, & PERCENTS

Math Preparation Guide

This guide provides an in-depth look at the variety of
GMAT questions that test your knowledge of fractions,
decimals, and percents. Learn to see the connections
among these part-whole relationships and practice
implementing strategic shortcuts.

Fractions, Decimals, and Percents GMAT Preparation Guide, 2007 Edition

10-digit International Standard Book Number: 0-9790175-1-3
13-digit International Standard Book Number: 978-0-9790175-1-3

Note: *GMAT, Graduate Management Admission Test, Graduate Management Admission Council,* and *GMAC* are all registered trademarks of the Graduate Management Admission Council which neither sponsors nor is affiliated in any way with this product.

8 GUIDE INSTRUCTIONAL SERIES

Math GMAT Preparation Guides

Number Properties (ISBN: 978-0-9790175-0-6)

Fractions, Decimals, & Percents (ISBN: 978-0-9790175-1-3)

Equations, Inequalities, & VIC's (ISBN: 978-0-9790175-2-0)

Word Translations (ISBN: 978-0-9790175-3-7)

Geometry (ISBN: 978-0-9790175-4-4)

Verbal GMAT Preparation Guides

Critical Reasoning (ISBN: 978-0-9790175-5-1)

Reading Comprehension (ISBN: 978-0-9790175-6-8)

Sentence Correction (ISBN: 978-0-9790175-7-5)

HOW OUR GMAT PREP BOOKS ARE DIFFERENT

One of our core beliefs at Manhattan GMAT is that a curriculum should be more than just a guidebook of tricks and tips. Scoring well on the GMAT requires a curriculum that builds true content knowledge and understanding. Skim through this guide and this is what you will see:

You will *not* find page after page of guessing techniques.

Instead, you will find a highly organized and structured guide that actually teaches you the content you need to know to do well on the GMAT.

You *will* find many more pages-per-topic than in all-in-one tomes.

Each chapter covers one specific topic area in-depth, explaining key concepts, detailing in-depth strategies, and building specific skills through Manhattan GMAT's *In-Action* problem sets (with comprehensive explanations). Why are there 8 guides? Each of the 8 books (5 Math, 3 Verbal) covers a major content area in extensive depth, allowing you to delve into each topic in great detail. In addition, you may purchase only those guides that pertain to those areas in which you need to improve.

This guide is challenging - it asks you to do more, not less.

It starts with the fundamental skills, but does not end there; it also includes the *most advanced content* that many other prep books ignore. As the average GMAT score required to gain admission to top business schools continues to rise, this guide, together with the 6 computer adaptive online practice exams and bonus question bank included with your purchase, provides test-takers with the depth and volume of advanced material essential for achieving the highest scores, given the GMAT's computer adaptive format.

This guide is ambitious - developing mastery is its goal.

Developed by Manhattan GMAT's staff of REAL teachers (all of whom have 99th percentile official GMAT scores), our ambitious curriculum seeks to provide test-takers of all levels with an in-depth and carefully tailored approach that enables our students to achieve mastery. If you are looking to learn more than just the "process of elimination" and if you want to develop skills, strategies, and a confident approach to any problem that you may see on the GMAT, then our sophisticated preparation guides are the tools to get you there.

HOW TO ACCESS YOUR ONLINE RESOURCES

Please read this entire page of information, all the way down to the bottom of the page! This page describes WHAT online resources are included with the purchase of this book and HOW to access these resources.

[**If you are a registered Manhattan GMAT student** and have received this book as part of your course materials, you have AUTOMATIC access to ALL of our online resources. This includes all simulated practice exams, question banks, and online updates to this book. To access these resources, follow the instructions in the Welcome Guide provided to you at the start of your program. Do NOT follow the instructions below.]

If you have purchased this book, your purchase includes 1 YEAR OF ONLINE ACCESS to the following:

6 Computer Adaptive Online Practice Exams

Bonus Online Question Bank for FRACTIONS, DECIMALS, & PERCENTS

Online Updates to the Content in this Book

The 6 full-length computer adaptive practice exams included with the purchase of this book are delivered online using Manhattan GMAT's proprietary computer adaptive online test engine. The exams adapt to your ability level by drawing from a bank of more than 1200 unique questions of varying difficulty levels written by Manhattan GMAT's expert instructors, all of whom have scored in the 99th percentile on the Official GMAT. At the end of each exam you will receive a score, an analysis of your results, and the opportunity to review detailed explanations for each question. You may choose to take the exams timed or untimed.

The Bonus Online Question Bank for Fractions, Decimals, & Percents consists of 25 extra practice questions (with detailed explanations) that test the variety of Fraction, Decimal, & Percent concepts and skills covered in this book. These questions provide you with extra practice *beyond* the problem sets contained in this book. You may use our online timer to practice your pacing by setting time limits for each question in the bank.

The content presented in this book is updated periodically to ensure that it reflects the GMAT's most current trends. You may view all updates, including any known errors or changes, upon registering for online access.

Important Note: The 6 computer adaptive online exams included with the purchase of this book are the SAME exams that you receive upon purchasing ANY book in Manhattan GMAT's 8 Book Preparation Series. On the other hand, the Bonus Online Question Bank for FRACTIONS, DECIMALS, & PERCENTS is a unique resource that you receive ONLY with the purchase of this specific title.

To access the online resources listed above, you will need this book in front of you and you will need to register your information online. This book includes access to the above resources for ONE PERSON ONLY.

To register and start using your online resources, please go online to the following URL:

http://www.manhattangmat.com/access.cfm (Double check that you have typed this in accurately!)

Your one-year of online access begins on the day that you register at the above URL. You only need to register your product ONCE at the above URL. To use your online resources any time AFTER you have completed the registration process, please login to the following URL:

http://www.manhattangmat.com/practicecenter.cfm

TABLE OF CONTENTS

g

Chapter 1
of
FRACTIONS, DECIMALS, & PERCENTS

DIGITS &
DECIMALS

In This Chapter . . .

DECIMALS

GMAT math goes beyond an understanding of the properties of integers or whole numbers. The GMAT also tests your ability to understand the numbers that fall in between the whole numbers. These numbers are called decimals.

For example, the decimal 6.3 falls between the integers 6 and 7.

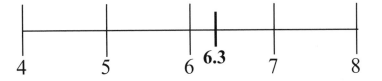

Some other examples of decimals include:

Decimals less than -1: $-3.65, -12.01, -145.9$
Decimals between -1 and 0: $-.65, -.8912, -.076$
Decimals between 0 and 1: $.65, .8912, .076$
Decimals greater than 1: $3.65, 12.01, 145.9$

Note that an integer can be expressed as a decimal by adding the decimal point and the number 0. For example:

   $8 = 8.0$ $123 = 123.0$ $400 = 400.0$

DIGITS

Every number is composed of digits. There are only ten digits in our number system: 0, 1, 2, 3, 4, 5, 6, 7, 8, 9. The term digit refers to one building block of a number; it does not refer to a number itself. For example:

356 is a number composed of three digits: 3, 5, and 6.

Numbers are often classified by the number of digits they contain. For example:

2, 7, and -8 are each single-digit numbers (they are each composed of one digit).
43, 63, and -14 are each double-digit numbers (composed of two digits).
100, 765 and -890 are each triple-digit numbers (composed of three digits).
500,000 and $-468,024$ are each six-digit numbers (composed of six digits).
789,526,622 is a nine-digit number (composed of nine digits).

Note that decimals can be classified by the number of digits they contain as well:

3.4 is a number that contains two digits.
7.05 is a number that contains three digits.
106.7559 is a number that contains seven digits.

You can use a number line to decide between which whole numbers a decimal falls.

Place Value

Every digit in a number has a particular place value depending on its location within the number. For example, in the number 452, the digit 2 is in the ones (or units) place, the digit 5 is in the tens place, and the digit 4 is in the hundreds place. The name of each location corresponds to the "value" of that place. Thus:

2 is worth two units, or 2.
5 is worth five tens, or 50.
4 is worth four hundreds, or 400.

You should memorize the names of all the place values.

6	9	2	5	6	7	8	9	1	0	2	3	.	8	3	4	7
HUNDRED	TEN	ONE	HUNDRED	TEN	ONE	HUNDRED	TEN		HUNDREDS	TENS	UNITS		TENTHS	HUNDREDTHS	THOUSANDTHS	TEN THOUSANDTHS
BILLIONS	BILLIONS	BILLIONS	MILLIONS	MILLIONS	MILLIONS	THOUSANDS	THOUSANDS	THOUSANDS								

The chart to the left analyzes the place value of all the digits in the number:

692,567,891,023.8347

Notice that the place values to the left of the decimal all end in "-s", while the place values to the right of the decimal all end in "-ths." This is because the suffix "-ths" gives these places (to the right of the decimal) a fractional value.

Let's analyze the end of the preceding number: **.8347**

8 is in the tenths place, giving it a value of 8 tenths, or $\dfrac{8}{10}$.

3 is in the hundredths place, giving it a value of 3 hundredths, or $\dfrac{3}{100}$.

4 is in the thousandths place, giving it a value of 4 thousandths, or $\dfrac{4}{1000}$.

7 is in the ten thousandths place, giving it a value of 7 ten thousandths, or $\dfrac{7}{10,000}$.

To use a concrete example, .8 means eight tenths of one dollar, which would be 8 dimes or 80 cents. Additionally, .03 means three hundredths of one dollar, which would be 3 pennies or 3 cents.

Using Place Value on the GMAT

You will never be asked to find the digit in the tens place on the GMAT. However, you will need to use place value to solve fairly difficult GMAT problems.

Consider the following problem:

> **A and B are both two-digit numbers. If A and B contain the same digits, but in reverse order, what integer must be a factor of (A + B)?**

To solve this problem, assign two variables to be the digits in A and B: x and y. Using your knowledge of place value, you can express A as $10x + y$, where x is the digit in the tens place and y is the digit in the units place. B, therefore, can be expressed as $10y + x$. The sum of A and B can be expressed as follows:

$$A + B = 10x + y + 10y + x = 11x + 11y = 11(x + y)$$

Clearly, 11 must be a factor of A + B.

Rounding to the Nearest Place Value

Knowing place value is important because the GMAT occasionally requires you to round a number to a specific place value. For example:

> **What is 3.681 rounded to the nearest tenth?**

First, find the digit located in the specified place value. The digit 6 is in the tenths place.

Second, look at the right-digit-neighbor (the digit immediately to the right) of the digit in question. In this case, 8 is the right-digit-neighbor of 6.

If the right-digit-neighbor is 5 or greater, round the digit in question UP. But if the right-digit-neighbor is 4 or less, the digit in question remains the same. In this case, since 8 is greater than five, the digit in question (6) must be rounded up to 7. Thus, 3.681 rounded to the nearest tenth equals 3.7.

Note that all the digits to the right of the right-digit-neighbor are irrelevant when rounding. In the last example, the digit 1 is not important.

Rounding appears on the GMAT in the form of questions like these:

> **If x is the decimal 8.1d5, and x rounded to the nearest tenth is equal to 8.1, which integers could not be the value of d?**

In order for x to be 8.1 when rounded to the nearest tenth, the right-digit neighbor, d, must be less than 5. Therefore d cannot be 5, 6, 7, 8 or 9.

Adding Zeroes to Decimals

Adding zeroes to the end of a decimal does not change the value of the decimal. For example: $3.6 = 3.60 = 3.6000$ & $65.689 = 65.68900 = 65.68900000$

Removing zeroes from the end of a decimal does not change the value of the decimal either: $3.600000 = 3.6$ & $65.68900000 = 65.689$

Be careful, however, not to add or remove any zeroes from within a number. Doing so will change the value of the number:
$7.01 \neq 7.1$ & $923.01 \neq 923.001$

Powers of 10: Shifting the Decimal

When you shift the decimal to the right, the number gets bigger. When you shift the decimal to the left, the number gets smaller.

Place values continually decrease from left to right by powers of 10. Understanding this can help you understand the following shortcuts for multiplication and division.

In words	thousands	hundreds	tens	ones	tenths	hundredths	thousandths
In numbers	1000	100	10	1	.1	.01	.001
In powers of ten	10^3	10^2	10^1	10^0	10^{-1}	10^{-2}	10^{-3}

When you multiply any number by a power of ten, move the decimal forward (right) the specified number of places:

$3.9742 \times 10^3 = 3974.2$ (Move the decimal forward 3 spaces.)
$89.507 \times 10 = 895.07$ (Move the decimal forward 1 space.)

When you divide any number by a power of ten, move the decimal backward (left) the specified number of places:

$4169.2 \div 10^2 = 41.692$ (Move the decimal backward 2 spaces.)
$89.507 \div 10 = 8.9507$ (Move the decimal backward 1 space.)

Note that if you need to add zeroes in order to shift a decimal, you should do so:

$2.57 \times 10^6 = 2,570,000$ (In order to move the decimal forward 6 spaces, add four zeroes to the end of the number.)
$14.29 \div 10^5 = .0001429$ (In order to move the decimal backward 5 spaces, add three zeroes to the beginning of the number.)

Finally, note that negative powers of ten reverse the regular process:

$6782.01 \times 10^{-3} = 6.78201$ (Moving the decimal forward by negative 3 spaces means moving it backward by 3 spaces.)
$53.0447 \div 10^{-2} = 5304.47$ (Moving the decimal backward by negative 2 spaces means moving it forward by 2 spaces.)

The Last Digit Shortcut

Consider this problem:

What is the units digit of $(5)^2(9)^2(4)^3$?

In this problem, you can use the Last Digit Shortcut. Solve the problem step by step. However, only pay attention to the last digit of every intermediate product. Drop any other digits.

STEP 1: $5 \times 5 = 25$ Drop the tens digit and keep only the last digit: 5.
STEP 2: $9 \times 9 = 81$ Drop the tens digit and keep only the last digit: 1.
STEP 3: $4 \times 4 \times 4 = 64$ Drop the tens digit and keep only the last digit: 4.
STEP 4: $5 \times 1 \times 4 = 20$ Multiply the last digits of each of the products.

The units digit of the final product is 0.

The Heavy Division Shortcut

Some division problems involving decimals can look rather complex. Often on the GMAT, you only need to find an approximate solution in order to answer a question. In these cases, you should save yourself time by using the heavy division shortcut. This shortcut employs the decimal-shifting rules you just learned.

What is $1,530,794 \div (31.49 \times 10^4)$ to the nearest whole number?

Since we are looking for an estimate, we can use the heavy division shortcut.

Step 1: Set up the division problem in fraction form:

$$\frac{1,530,794}{31.49 \times 10^4}$$

Step 2: Rewrite the problem, eliminating powers of 10:

$$\frac{1,530,794}{314,900}$$

Step 3: Your goal is to get a single digit to the left of the decimal in the denominator. In this problem, you need to move the decimal point backward 5 spaces. You can do this to the denominator as long as you do the same thing to the numerator.

$$\frac{1,530,794}{314,900} = \frac{15.30794}{3.14900}$$

Now you have the single digit 3 to the left of the decimal in the denominator.

Step 4: Focus only on the whole number parts of the numerator and denominator and solve.

$$\frac{15.30794}{3.14900} \approx \frac{15}{3} = 5$$

An approximate answer to the complex division problem is 5.

Use the Heavy Division Shortcut when you need an approximate answer.

Decimal Operations

ADDITION AND SUBTRACTION

To add or subtract decimals, make sure to line up the decimal points. Then add zeroes to make the right sides of the decimals the same length.

4.319 + 221.8

Line up the	4.319
decimal points	+ 221.800
and add zeroes.	226.119

10 − .063

Line up the	10.000
decimal points	− .063
and add zeroes.	9.937

Addition & Subtraction: Line up the decimal points!

> The rules for decimal operations are different for each operation.

MULTIPLICATION

To multiply decimals, ignore the decimal point until the end. Just multiply the numbers as you would if they were whole numbers. Then count the *total* number of digits to the right of the decimal point in the factors. The product should have the same number of digits to the right of the decimal point.

.02 × 1.4

Multiply normally:

14
× 2
28

There are 3 digits to the right of the decimal point in the factors (0 and 2 in the first factor and 4 in the second factor). Therefore, move the decimal point 3 places to the left in the product: $28 \rightarrow .028$

Multiplication: Conserve digits to the right of the decimal point!

DIVISION

If there is a decimal point in the dividend (the inner number) only, you can simply bring the decimal point up and divide normally.

Ex. **12.42 ÷ 3** = 4.14

```
      4.14
3)12.42
    12
    04
     3
    12
```

However, if there is a decimal point in the divisor (the outer number), you should shift the decimal point in both the divisor and the dividend to make the *divisor* a whole number. Then, bring the decimal point up and divide.

Ex: **12.42 ÷ .3** → 124.2 ÷ 3 = 41.4

```
      41.4
3)124.2
    12
    04
     3
    12
```

Move the decimal one space to the right to make .3 a whole number. Then, move the decimal one space in 12.42 to make it 124.2.

You can always simplify division problems that involve decimals by shifting the decimal point in both the divisor and the dividend, even when the division problem is expressed as a fraction:

$$\frac{.0045}{.09} = \frac{45}{900}$$

Move the decimal 4 spaces to the right to make both the numerator and the denominator whole numbers.

Note that this is essentially the same process as simplifying a fraction. You are simply multiplying the numerator and denominator of the fraction by a power of ten—in this case, 10^4, or 10,000.

Remember, in order to divide decimals, you must make the OUTER number a whole number by shifting the decimal point.

Problem Set

Solve each problem, applying the concepts and rules you learned in this section.

1.   What is the units digit of $(2)^5(3)^3(4)^2$?

2.   What is the sum of all the possible 3-digit numbers that can be constructed using the digits 3, 4, and 5, if each digit can be used only once in each number?

3.   In the decimal, 2.4d7, d represents a digit from 0-9. If the value of the decimal rounded to the nearest tenth is less than 2.5, what are the possible values of d?

4.   If k is an integer, and if $.02468 \times 10^k$ is greater than 10,000, what is the least possible value of k?

5.   Which integer values of b would give the number $2002 \div 10^{-b}$ a value between 1 and 100?

6.   Estimate: $\dfrac{4,509,982,344}{5.342 \times 10^4}$

7.   Simplify: $(4.5 \times 2 + 6.6) \div .003$

8.   Simplify: $(4 \times 10^{-2}) - (2.5 \times 10^{-3})$

9.   What is $4,563,021 \div 10^5$, rounded to the nearest whole number?

10.   Simplify: $(.08)^2 \div .4$

11.   If k is an integer, and if 422.93×10^k is less than 3, what is the greatest possible value of k?

12.   Simplify: $[8 - (1.08 + 6.9)]^2$

13.   Which integer values of j would give the number $-3,712 \times 10^j$ a value between -100 and -1?

14.   What is the units digit of $\left(\dfrac{6^6}{6^5}\right)^6$?

15.   Simplify: $\dfrac{.00081}{.09}$

1. **4:** Use the Last Digit Shortcut, ignoring all digits but the last in any intermediate products:

STEP ONE: $2^5 = 32$	Drop the tens digit and keep only the last digit: 2.
STEP TWO: $3^3 = 27$	Drop the tens digit and keep only the last digit: 7.
STEP THREE: $4^2 = 16$	Drop the tens digit and keep only the last digit: 6.
STEP FOUR: $2 \times 7 \times 6 = 84$	Drop the tens digit and keep only the last digit: 4.

2. **2664:** There are 6 ways in which to arrange these digits: 345, 354, 435, 453, 534, and 543. Notice that each digit appears twice in the hundreds column, twice in the tens column, and twice in the ones column. Therefore, you can use your knowledge of place value to find the sum quickly:
$$100(24) + 10(24) + (24) = 2400 + 240 + 24 = 2664.$$

3. **{0, 1, 2, 3, 4}:** If d is 5 or greater, the decimal rounded to the nearest tenth will be 2.5.

4. **6:** Multiplying .02468 by a positive power of ten will shift the decimal point to the right. Simply shift the decimal point to the right until the result is greater than 10,000. Keep track of how many times you shift the decimal point. Shifting the decimal point 5 times results in 2,468. This is still less than 10,000. Shifting one more place yields 24,680, which is greater than 10,000.

5. **{−2, −3}:** In order to give 2002 a value between 1 and 100, we must shift the decimal point to change the number to 2.002 or 20.02. This requires a shift of either two or three places to the left. Remember that, while multiplication shifts the decimal point to the right, division shifts it to the left. To shift the decimal point 2 places to the left, we would divide by 10^2. To shift it 3 places to the left, we would divide by 10^3. Therefore, the exponent $-b = \{2, 3\}$, and $b = \{-2, -3\}$.

6. **90,000:** Use the Heavy Division Shortcut to estimate:
$$\frac{4,509,982,344}{53,420} = \frac{4,500,000,000}{50,000} = \frac{450,000}{5} = 90,000$$

7. **5,200:** Use the order of operations, PEMDAS (Parentheses, Exponents, Multiplication & Division, Addition and Subtraction) to simplify.
$$\frac{9 + 6.6}{.003} = \frac{15.6}{.003} = \frac{15,600}{3} = 5,200$$

8. **.0375:** First, rewrite the numbers in standard notation by shifting the decimal point. Then, add zeroes, line up the decimal points, and subtract.

$$\begin{array}{r} .0400 \\ - .0025 \\ \hline .0375 \end{array}$$

9. **46:** To divide by a positive power of 10, shift the decimal point to the left. This yields 45.63021. To round to the nearest whole number, look at the tenths place. The digit in the tenths place, 6, is more than five. Therefore, the number is closest to 46.

10. **.016:** Use the order of operations, PEMDAS (Parentheses, Exponents, Multiplication & Division, Addition and Subtraction) to simplify.

$$\frac{(0.08)^2}{.4} = \frac{.0064}{.4} = \frac{.064}{4} = .016$$

11. **−3:** Multiplying 422.93 by a negative power of ten will shift the decimal point to the left. Simply shift the decimal point to the left until the result is less than 3. Keep track of how many times you shift the decimal point. Shifting the decimal point 2 times results in 4.2293. This is still more than 3. Shifting one more place yields .42293, which is less than 3.

12. **.0004:** Use the order of operations, PEMDAS (Parentheses, Exponents, Multiplication & Division, Addition and Subtraction) to simplify.

First, add 1.08 + 6.9 by lining up the decimal points:

$$\begin{array}{r} 1.08 \\ + 6.9 \\ \hline 7.98 \end{array}$$

Then, subtract 7.98 from 8 by lining up the decimal points, adding zeroes to make the decimals the same length:

$$\begin{array}{r} 8.00 \\ - 7.98 \\ \hline .02 \end{array}$$

Finally, square .02, conserving the number of digits to the right of the decimal point.

$$\begin{array}{r} .02 \\ \times .02 \\ \hline .0004 \end{array}$$

13. **{−2, −3}:** In order to give −3,712 a value between −100 and −1, we must shift the decimal point to change the number to −37.12 or −3.712. This requires a shift of either two or three places to the left. Remember that, while multiplication shifts the decimal point to the right, division shifts it to the left. To shift the decimal point 2 places to the left, we would multiply by 10^{-2}. To shift it 3 places to the left, we would multiply by 10^{-3}. Therefore, the exponent $j = \{-2, -3\}$.

14. **6:** First, use the rules for combining exponents to simplify the expression $\frac{6^6}{6^5}$. To combine exponents in division, subtract the exponents. Therefore, $\frac{6^6}{6^5} = 6$. Then, raise this to the sixth power:

$$6^6 = 6^2 \times 6^2 \times 6^2 = 36 \times 36 \times 36.$$

Ignore any digits other than the last one: $6 \times 6 \times 6 = 36 \times 6$. Again, ignore any digits other than the last one: $6 \times 6 = 36$. The last digit is 6.

15. **.009:** Shift the decimal point 2 spaces to eliminate the decimal point in the denominator. Then divide, either mentally or using long division.

$$\frac{.00081}{.09} = \frac{.081}{9}$$

$$\begin{array}{r} .009 \\ 9\overline{)\,.081} \\ \underline{0} \\ 08 \\ \underline{0} \\ 81 \\ \underline{81} \\ 0 \end{array}$$

Chapter 2
of
FRACTIONS, DECIMALS, & PERCENTS

FRACTIONS

In This Chapter . . .

- Numerator and Denominator Rules
- Simplifying Proper Fractions
- Simplifying Improper Fractions
- The Multiplication Shortcut
- No Addition or Subtraction Shortcuts
- Dividing Fractions: Use the Reciprocal
- Division in Disguise
- Fraction Operations: Funky Results
- Comparing Fractions: Cross-Multiply
- Never Split the Denominator
- Benchmark Values
- Smart Numbers: Multiples of the Denominators
- When Not to Use Smart Numbers

FRACTIONS

Decimals are one way of expressing the numbers that fall in between the whole numbers. Another way of expressing these numbers is through fractions.

For example, the fraction $6\frac{1}{2}$ falls between the integers 6 and 7.

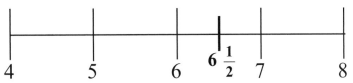

Proper fractions are those that fall between 0 and 1. In proper fractions, the numerator is always smaller than the denominator. For example:

$$\frac{1}{4}, \frac{1}{2}, \frac{2}{3}, \frac{7}{10}$$

Improper fractions are those that are greater than 1. In improper fractions, the numerator is greater than the denominator. For example:

$$\frac{5}{4}, \frac{13}{2}, \frac{11}{3}, \frac{101}{10}$$

Improper fractions can be rewritten as mixed numbers. A mixed number is an integer and a proper fraction. For example:

$$\frac{5}{4} = 1\frac{1}{4} \qquad\qquad \frac{13}{2} = 6\frac{1}{2} \qquad\qquad \frac{11}{3} = 3\frac{2}{3} \qquad\qquad \frac{101}{10} = 10\frac{1}{10}$$

Although all the preceding examples use positive fractions, note that fractions can be negative as well.

Proper and improper fractions behave differently in many cases.

Numerator and Denominator Rules

Certain key rules govern the relationship between the numerator (the top number) and the denominator (the bottom number) of proper fractions. These rules are important to internalize, but keep in mind that they **only apply to positive proper fractions (fractions between 0 and 1).**

As the NUMERATOR goes up, the fraction INCREASES. If you increase the numerator of a fraction, while holding the denominator constant, the fraction increases in value as it approaches 1.

$$\frac{1}{8} < \frac{2}{8} < \frac{3}{8} < \frac{4}{8} < \frac{5}{8} < \frac{6}{8} < \frac{7}{8} < \frac{8}{8} = 1$$

As the DENOMINATOR goes up, the fraction DECREASES. If you increase the denominator of a fraction, while holding the numerator constant, the fraction decreases in value as it approaches 0.

$$\frac{1}{2} > \frac{1}{3} > \frac{1}{4} > \frac{1}{5} > \frac{1}{6} \dots > \frac{1}{1000} \approx 0$$

Increasing BOTH the numerator and the denominator by THE SAME VALUE brings the fraction closer to 1. If you add the same number to both the numerator and the denominator, the fraction increases in value as it approaches 1.

$$\frac{1}{2} < \frac{1+1}{2+1} = \frac{2}{3} < \frac{2+9}{3+9} = \frac{11}{12} < \frac{11+1000}{12+1000} = \frac{1011}{1012}$$

Thus: $\dfrac{1}{2} < \dfrac{2}{3} < \dfrac{11}{12} < \dfrac{1011}{1012} \approx 1$

These rules only apply to positive proper fractions!

Simplifying Proper Fractions

Simplifying fractions is a process that attempts to express a fraction in its lowest terms. The process of simplifying is governed by one simple rule:

MULTIPLYING or DIVIDING both the numerator and the denominator by the same number does not change the value of the fraction.

$$\frac{4}{5} = \frac{4(3)}{5(3)} = \frac{12}{15} = \frac{12(2)}{15(2)} = \frac{24}{30} \qquad \frac{24}{30} = \frac{24 \div 2}{30 \div 2} = \frac{12}{15} = \frac{12 \div 3}{15 \div 3} = \frac{4}{5}$$

Simplifying a fraction means dividing both the numerator and the denominator by a common factor. This must be repeated until no common factors remain.

$$\frac{20}{30} \rightarrow \frac{20 \div 5}{30 \div 5} = \frac{4}{6} \quad \text{(Numerator and denominator are divided by the common factor 5.)}$$

$$\frac{4}{6} \rightarrow \frac{4 \div 2}{6 \div 2} = \frac{2}{3} \quad \text{(Numerator and denominator are divided by the common factor 2.)}$$

There are no more common factors, so $\frac{20}{30}$ has been fully simplified to $\frac{2}{3}$.

Alternatively, we could have simplified $\frac{20}{30}$ in only one step by dividing both the

numerator and denominator by their greatest common factor (10) to yield $\frac{2}{3}$.

Simplify fractions by multiplying or dividing both the numerator and the denominator by the same number.

Converting Improper Fractions to Mixed Numbers

To convert an improper fraction into a mixed number, simply divide the numerator by the denominator, stopping when you reach a remainder smaller than the denominator.

$$\frac{9}{4} = 9 \div 4 = 4\overline{)9}$$
$$\underline{8}$$
$$1$$

Since $9 \div 4$ equals 2 with a remainder of 1, we can write the improper fraction as the integer 2 with a fractional part of 1 over the original denominator of 4.

Thus, $\frac{9}{4} = 2\frac{1}{4}$.

This process can also work in reverse. In order to convert a mixed number into an improper fraction (something you need to do in order to multiply or divide mixed numbers), use the following procedure:

$2\frac{1}{4}$ Multiply the denominator (4) by the whole number (2) and add the numerator (1): $4 \times 2 + 1 = 9$.

$\frac{9}{4}$ Place the number 9 over the original denominator, 4.

The Multiplication Shortcut

To multiply fractions, first multiply the numerators together, then multiply the denominators together, and finally simplify your resulting product by expressing it in lowest terms. For example:

$$\frac{8}{15} \times \frac{35}{72} = \frac{8(35)}{15(72)} = \frac{280}{1080} = \frac{28}{108} = \frac{7}{27}$$

There is, however, a shortcut that can make fraction multiplication much less tedious. The shortcut is to simplify your products BEFORE multiplying. This is also known as "cancelling."

Notice that the **8** in the numerator and the **72** in the denominator both have 8 as a factor. Thus, they can be simplified from $\frac{8}{72}$ to $\frac{1}{9}$.

Notice also that **35** in the numerator and **15** in the denominator both have 5 as a factor. Thus, they can be simplified from $\frac{35}{15}$ to $\frac{7}{3}$.

Now the multiplication will be easier and no further simplification will be necessary:

$$\frac{8}{15} \times \frac{35}{72} = \frac{8(35)}{15(72)} = \frac{1(7)}{3(9)} = \frac{7}{27}$$

In order to multiply mixed numbers, you must first convert each mixed number into an improper fraction:

$$2\frac{1}{3} \times 6\frac{3}{5} = \frac{7}{3} \times \frac{33}{5}$$

You can simplify the problem, using the multiplication shortcut of cancelling, and then convert the result to a mixed number:

$$\frac{7}{3} \times \frac{33}{5} = \frac{7(33)}{3(5)} = \frac{7(11)}{1(5)} = \frac{77}{5} = 15\frac{2}{5}$$

No Addition or Subtraction Shortcuts

While shortcuts are very useful when multiplying fractions, you must be careful NOT to take any shortcuts when adding or subtracting fractions. In order to add or subtract fractions, you must:

(1) find a common denominator
(2) change each fraction so that it is expressed using this common denominator
(3) add up the numerators only

$$\frac{3}{8} + \frac{7}{12}$$

A common denominator is 24. Thus, $\frac{3}{8} = \frac{9}{24}$ and $\frac{7}{12} = \frac{14}{24}$.

$$\frac{9}{24} + \frac{14}{24}$$

Express each fraction using the common denominator 24.

$$\frac{9}{24} + \frac{14}{24} = \frac{23}{24}$$

Finally, add the numerators to find the answer.

Another example:

$$\frac{11}{15} - \frac{7}{30}$$

A common denominator is 30. $\frac{11}{15} = \frac{22}{30}$ and $\frac{7}{30}$ stays the same.

$$\frac{22}{30} - \frac{7}{30}$$

Express each fraction using the common denominator 30.

$$\frac{22}{30} - \frac{7}{30} = \frac{15}{30}$$

Subtract the numerators.

$$\frac{15}{30} = \frac{1}{2}$$

Simplify $\frac{15}{30}$ to find the answer.

> To add and subtract fractions, you must find a common denominator.

In order to add or subtract mixed numbers, set up the problem vertically and solve the fraction first and the whole number last.

Addition

$$7\frac{1}{3} = 7\frac{2}{6}$$
$$+ \ 4\frac{1}{2} = 4\frac{3}{6}$$
$$\overline{11\frac{5}{6}}$$

Subtraction

$$7\frac{1}{3} = 7\frac{2}{6} = 6\frac{8}{6}$$
$$- \ 4\frac{1}{2} = 4\frac{3}{6} = 4\frac{3}{6}$$
$$\overline{2\frac{5}{6}}$$

Notice the reason for starting with the fraction. You may need to borrow from the whole number, as in this example. Here, the top number "borrows" a whole number (worth 6 parts), thus increasing its numerator from 2 to 8 (making it bigger than the 3 numerator of the bottom fraction).

Dividing Fractions: Use the Reciprocal

In order to divide fractions, you must first understand the concept of the reciprocal. You can think of the reciprocal as the fraction flipped upside down.

The reciprocal of $\frac{3}{4}$ is $\frac{4}{3}$.   The reciprocal of $\frac{2}{9}$ is $\frac{9}{2}$.

What is the reciprocal of an integer? Think of an integer as a fraction with a denominator of 1. Thus, the integer 5 is really just $\frac{5}{1}$. To find the reciprocal, just flip it.

The reciprocal of **5** or $\frac{5}{1}$ is $\frac{1}{5}$.   The reciprocal of **8** is $\frac{1}{8}$.

To check if you have found the reciprocal of a number, use this rule: **The product of a number and its reciprocal always equals 1.** The following examples reveal this to be true:

$$\frac{3}{4} \times \frac{4}{3} = \frac{12}{12} = 1 \qquad 5 \times \frac{1}{5} = \frac{5}{1} \times \frac{1}{5} = \frac{5}{5} = 1 \qquad \sqrt{7} \times \frac{\sqrt{7}}{7} = \frac{\sqrt{7}}{1} \times \frac{\sqrt{7}}{7} = \frac{7}{7} = 1$$

In order to divide fractions,
      (1) change the divisor into its reciprocal, and then
      (2) multiply the fractions. Note that the divisor is the second number:

$$\frac{1}{2} \div \frac{3}{4}$$

First, change the divisor $\frac{3}{4}$ into its reciprocal $\frac{4}{3}$.

$$\frac{1}{2} \times \frac{4}{3} = \frac{4}{6} = \frac{2}{3}$$

Then, multiply the fractions and simplify to lowest terms.

In order to divide mixed numbers, first change them into improper fractions:

$$5\frac{2}{3} \div 8\frac{1}{2} = \frac{17}{3} \div \frac{17}{2}$$

Then, change the divisor $\frac{17}{2}$ into its reciprocal $\frac{2}{17}$.

$$\frac{17}{3} \times \frac{2}{17} = \frac{2}{3}$$

Multiply the fractions, cancelling where you can.

To divide fractions, flip the second fraction and multiply.

Division in Disguise

Sometimes, dividing fractions can be written in a confusing way. Consider one of the previous examples:

$\dfrac{1}{2} \div \dfrac{3}{4}$ can also be written this way: $\dfrac{\dfrac{1}{2}}{\dfrac{3}{4}}$

Do not be confused. When a fraction is written with four terms, just rewrite it as the top fraction divided by the bottom fraction, and solve it normally (by using the reciprocal of the divisor and then multiplying).

Multiplying and dividing positive proper fractions yields unexpected results.

$$\dfrac{\dfrac{1}{2}}{\dfrac{3}{4}} = \dfrac{1}{2} \div \dfrac{3}{4} = \dfrac{1}{2} \times \dfrac{4}{3} = \dfrac{4}{6} = \dfrac{2}{3}$$

Fraction Operations: Funky Results

Performing basic operations—addition, subtraction, multiplication, and division—on proper fractions (those between 0 and 1) yields some unexpected results. Consider the following chart:

OPERATION	EXAMPLE	INCREASE OR DECREASE
Adding Fractions	$\dfrac{3}{5} + \dfrac{1}{5} = \dfrac{4}{5}$	INCREASE: Similar to adding positive integers, adding fractions increases their value.
Subtracting Fractions	$\dfrac{3}{5} - \dfrac{1}{5} = \dfrac{2}{5}$	DECREASE: Similar to subtracting positive integers, subtracting fractions decreases their value.
Multiplying Fractions	$\dfrac{3}{5} \times \dfrac{1}{5} = \dfrac{3}{25}$	**DECREASE:** Unlike multiplying positive integers, multiplying fractions decreases their value.
Dividing Fractions	$\dfrac{3}{5} \div \dfrac{1}{5} = \dfrac{3}{5} \times \dfrac{5}{1} = 3$	**INCREASE:** Unlike dividing positive integers, dividing fractions increases their value.

Note that multiplying proper fractions decreases their value, while dividing proper fractions increases their value—exactly the opposite of what happens with integers. The GMAT sometimes tests whether you remember this important difference between fractions and integers.

Comparing Fractions: Cross-Multiply

Which fraction is greater, $\dfrac{7}{9}$ or $\dfrac{4}{5}$?

The traditional method of comparing fractions involves finding a common denominator and comparing the two fractions. The common denominator of 9 and 5 is 45.

Thus, $\dfrac{7}{9} = \dfrac{35}{45}$ and $\dfrac{4}{5} = \dfrac{36}{45}$. We can see that $\dfrac{4}{5}$ is slightly bigger than $\dfrac{7}{9}$.

However, there is a shortcut to comparing fractions, called cross-multiplication. This is a process that involves multiplying the numerator of one fraction with the denominator of the other fraction, and vice versa:

Cross-multiplication can help you compare sets of several fractions.

$$\dfrac{7}{9} \quad\diagdown\!\!\!\!\diagup\quad \dfrac{4}{5}$$ Set up the fractions next to each other.

$\begin{array}{cc} (7 \times 5) & (4 \times 9) \\ 35 & 36 \end{array}$ Cross-multiply the fractions and put each answer under the corresponding <u>numerator</u> (NOT the denominator!)

$\dfrac{7}{9} \quad < \quad \dfrac{4}{5}$ Since 35 is less than 36, the first fraction must be less than the second one.

This process can save you a lot of time when comparing fractions (usually more than two!) on the GMAT.

Never Split the Denominator

One final rule, perhaps the most important one, is one that you must always remember when working with complex fractions. A complex fraction is a fraction in which there is a sum or a difference in the numerator or the denominator. Three examples of complex fractions are:

a) $\dfrac{15 + 10}{5}$ b) $\dfrac{5}{15 + 10}$ c) $\dfrac{15 + 10}{5 + 2}$

In example a), the numerator is expressed as a sum.
In example b), the denominator is expressed as a sum.
In example c), both the numerator and the denominator are expressed as sums.

When simplifying fractions that incorporate sums or differences, remember this rule: You may split up the terms of the numerator, but you may NEVER split the terms of the DENOMINATOR.

Thus, the terms in example a) may be split:

$$\frac{15 + 10}{5} = \frac{15}{5} + \frac{10}{5} = 3 + 2 = 5$$

But the terms in example b) may not be split:

$$\frac{5}{15+10} \neq \frac{5}{15} + \frac{5}{10} \quad \textbf{NO!}$$

Instead, simplify the denominator first:

$$\frac{5}{15 + 10} = \frac{5}{25} = \frac{1}{5}$$

The terms in example c) may not be split either:

$$\frac{15 + 10}{5 + 2} \neq \frac{15}{5} + \frac{10}{2} \quad \textbf{NO!}$$

Instead, simplify both parts of the fraction:

$$\frac{15 + 10}{5 + 2} = \frac{25}{7} = 3\,\frac{4}{7}$$

You can NEVER split the denominator!

Often, GMAT problems will involve complex fractions with variables. On these problems, it is tempting to split the denominator. Do not fall for it!

It is tempting to perform the following simplification:

$$\frac{\mathbf{5x - 2y}}{\mathbf{x - y}} = \frac{5x}{x} - \frac{2y}{y} = 5 - 2 = 3$$

But this is **WRONG** because you cannot split a difference in the denominator.

The reality is that $\dfrac{5x - 2y}{x - y}$ cannot be simplified further.

On the other hand, the expression $\dfrac{\mathbf{5x^2y - 2xy}}{\mathbf{xy}}$ can be simplified by splitting the

difference, because this difference appears in the numerator.

Thus: $\dfrac{5x^2y - 2xy}{xy} = \dfrac{5x^2y}{xy} - \dfrac{2xy}{xy} = 5x - 2 \quad$ (assuming $xy \neq 0$)

Benchmark Values

You will use a variety of estimating strategies on the GMAT. One important strategy for estimating with fractions is to use Benchmark Values. These are simple fractions with which you are already familiar:

$$\frac{1}{4}, \frac{1}{3}, \frac{1}{2}, \frac{2}{3}, \text{ and } \frac{3}{4}$$

You can use Benchmark Values to compare fractions:

Which is greater: $\dfrac{127}{255}$ or $\dfrac{162}{320}$?

If you recognize that 127 is less than half of 255, and 162 is more than half of 320, you will save yourself a lot of cumbersome computation.

You can also use Benchmark Values to estimate computations involving fractions:

What is $\dfrac{10}{22}$ of $\dfrac{5}{18}$ of 2000?

If you recognize that these fractions are very close to the Benchmark Values $\dfrac{1}{2}$ and $\dfrac{1}{4}$, you can estimate:

$$\frac{1}{2} \text{ of } \frac{1}{4} \text{ of } 2000 = 250. \text{ Therefore, } \frac{10}{22} \text{ of } \frac{5}{18} \text{ of } 2000 \approx 250.$$

When you find seemingly complicated fractions on the GMAT, use Benchmark Values to make sense of them.

Smart Numbers: Multiples of the Denominators

Sometimes, fraction problems on the GMAT include unspecified numerical amounts; often these unspecified amounts are described by variables. In these cases, pick real numbers to stand in for the variables. To make the computation easier, choose **Smart Numbers** equal to common multiples of the denominators of the fractions in the problem.

For example, consider this problem:

> **The Crandalls' hot tub is half filled. Their swimming pool, which has a capacity four times that of the tub, is filled to four-fifths of its capacity. If the hot tub is drained into the swimming pool, to what fraction of its capacity will the pool be filled?**

The denominators in this problem are 2 and 5. The Smart Number is the least common denominator, which is 10. Therefore, assign the hot tub a capacity of 10. Since the swimming pool has a capacity 4 times that of the pool, the swimming pool has a capacity of 40. We know that the hot tub is only half filled; therefore, it has 5 units of water in it. The swimming pool is four-fifths of the way filled, so it has 32 units of water in it.

Let's add the 5 units of water from the hot tub to the 32 units of water that are already in the swimming pool: 32 + 5 = 37.

With 37 units of water and a total capacity of 40, the pool will be filled to $\frac{37}{40}$ of its total capacity.

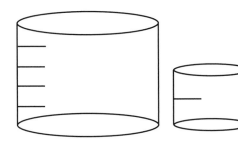

swimming pool
capacity: 40
filled: 32

hot tub
capacity: 10
filled: 5

You can often use Smart Numbers to help you solve problems with unspecified amounts.

When Not to Use Smart Numbers

In some problems, even though an amount might be unknown to you, it is actually specified in the problem in another way. In these cases, you cannot use Smart Numbers to assign real numbers to the variables. For example, consider this problem:

> **Mark's comic book collection contains 1/3 Killer Fish comics and 3/8 Shazaam Woman comics. The remainder of his collection consists of Boom! comics. If Mark has 70 Boom! comics, how many comics does he have in his entire collection?**

If there is even 1 specified amount in a problem, you cannot use Smart Numbers to solve it.

Even though you do not know the number of comics in Mark's collection, you can see that the total is not completely unspecified. You know a piece of the total: 70 Boom! comics. You can use this information to find the total. Do not use Smart Numbers here. Instead, solve similar problems by figuring out how big the known piece is; then, use that knowledge to find the size of the whole:

$$\frac{1}{3} \text{ Killer Fish} + \frac{3}{8} \text{ Shazaam Woman} = \frac{17}{24} \text{ comics that are not Boom!}$$

Therefore, $\frac{7}{24}$ of the comics are Boom! comics.

$$\frac{7}{24}x = 70$$

$$x = 70 \times \frac{24}{7}$$

$$x = 240$$

Mark has 240 comics.

Problem Set

For problems #1-5, decide whether the given operation will yield an INCREASE, a DECREASE, or a result that will STAY THE SAME.

1. Multiply the numerator of a positive, proper fraction by $\frac{3}{2}$.

2. Add 1 to the numerator of a positive, proper fraction and subtract 1 from its denominator.

3. Multiply both the numerator and denominator of a positive, proper fraction by $3\frac{1}{2}$.

4. Multiply a positive, proper fraction by $\frac{3}{8}$.

5. Divide a positive, proper fraction by $\frac{3}{13}$.

Solve problems #6-15.

6. Simplify: $\dfrac{10x}{5+x}$

7. Simplify: $\dfrac{8(3)(x)^2(3)}{6x}$

8. Simplify: $\dfrac{\frac{3}{5}+\frac{1}{3}}{\frac{2}{3}+\frac{2}{5}}$

9. Simplify: $\dfrac{12ab^3 - 6a^2b}{3ab}$ (given that $ab \neq 0$)

10. Put these fractions in order from least to greatest: $\dfrac{9}{17}$ $\dfrac{3}{16}$ $\dfrac{19}{20}$ $\dfrac{7}{15}$

11. Put these fractions in order from least to greatest: $\dfrac{2}{3}$ $\dfrac{3}{13}$ $\dfrac{5}{7}$ $\dfrac{2}{9}$

12. LuAnn spends 3/8 of her monthly paycheck on rent and 5/12 on food. Her roommate, Carrie, who earns twice as much as LuAnn, spends 1/4 of her monthly paycheck on rent and 1/2 on food. If the two women decide to donate the remainder of their money to charity each month, what fraction of their combined monthly income will they donate?

13.   Dujuan spends 1/2 of his monthly paycheck, after taxes, on rent. He spends 1/3 on food and 1/8 on entertainment. If he donates the entire remainder, $500.00, to charity, what is Dujuan's **annual** income, after taxes?

14.   Are $\dfrac{\sqrt{3}}{2}$ and $\dfrac{2\sqrt{3}}{3}$ reciprocals?

15.   Estimate: What is $\dfrac{11}{30}$ of $\dfrac{6}{20}$ of 120?

1. **INCREASE:** Multiplying the numerator of a positive fraction increases the numerator. As the numerator of a positive, proper fraction increases, its value increases.

2. **INCREASE:** As the numerator of a positive, proper fraction increases, the value of the fraction increases. As the denominator of a positive, proper fraction decreases, the value of the fraction also increases. Both actions will work to increase the value of the fraction.

3. **STAY THE SAME:** Multiplying or dividing the numerator and denominator of a fraction by the same number will not change the value of the fraction.

4. **DECREASE:** Multiplying a positive number by a proper fraction decreases the number.

5. **INCREASE:** Dividing a positive number by a positive, proper fraction increases the number.

6. **CANNOT SIMPLIFY:** There is no way to simplify this fraction; it is already in simplest form. Remember, you cannot split the denominator!

7. **12x:** First, combine terms in the numerator. Then, cancel terms in both the numerator and denominator.

$$\frac{72x^2}{6x} = 12x$$

8. **7/8:** To save time, multiply each of the small fractions by 15, which is the common denominator of all the fractions in the problem. Because we are multiplying the numerator *and* the denominator of the whole complex fraction by 15, we are not changing its value.

$$\frac{9+5}{10+6} = \frac{14}{16} = \frac{7}{8}$$

9. **2($2b^2 - a$) or $4b^2 - 2a$:** First, factor out common terms in the numerator. Then, cancel terms in both the numerator and denominator.

$$\frac{6ab(2b^2 - a)}{3ab} = 2(2b^2 - a) \text{ or } 4b^2 - 2a$$

10. **3/16 $<$ 7/15 $<$ 9/17 $<$ 19/20:** Use Benchmark Values to compare these fractions.

     9/17 is slightly more than 1/2. (8.5/17 would be exactly 1/2.)
     3/16 is slightly less than 1/4. (4/16 would be exactly 1/4.)
     19/20 is slightly less than 1. (20/20 would be exactly 1.)
     7/15 is slightly less than 1/2. (7.5/15 would be exactly 1/2.)

This makes it easy to order the fractions: 3/16 $<$ 7/15 $<$ 9/17 $<$ 19/20.

11. **2/9 < 3/13 < 2/3 < 5/7:** Using Benchmark Values, you should notice that 3/13 and 2/9 are both less than 1/2. 2/3 and 5/7 are both more than 1/2. Use cross-multiplication to compare each pair of fractions:

$$3 \times 9 = 27 \qquad \frac{3}{13} \qquad \frac{2}{9} \qquad 2 \times 13 = 26 \qquad \frac{3}{13} > \frac{2}{9}$$

$$2 \times 7 = 14 \qquad \frac{2}{3} \qquad \frac{5}{7} \qquad 5 \times 3 = 15 \qquad \frac{2}{3} < \frac{5}{7}$$

This makes it easy to order the fractions: $\dfrac{2}{9} < \dfrac{3}{13} < \dfrac{2}{3} < \dfrac{5}{7}$.

12. **17/72:** Use Smart Numbers to solve this problem. Since the denominators in the problem are 8, 12, 4, and 2, assign LuAnn a monthly paycheck of $24. Assign her roommate, who earns twice as much, a monthly paycheck of $48. The two women's monthly expenses break down as follows:

	Rent	Food	Leftover
LuAnn	3/8 of 24 = 9	5/12 of 24 = 10	24 − (9 + 10) = 5
Carrie	1/4 of 48 = 12	1/2 of 48 = 24	48 − (12 + 24) = 12

The women will donate a total of $17, out of their combined monthly income of $72.

13. **$144,000.00:** You cannot use Smart Numbers in this problem, because the total amount is specified. Even though the exact figure is not given in the problem, a portion of the total is specified. This means that the total is a certain number, although you do not know what it is. In fact, the total is exactly what you are being asked to find. Clearly, if you assign a number to represent the total, you will not be able to accurately find the total.

First, use addition to find the fraction of Dujuan's money that he spends on rent, food, and entertainment: 1/2 + 1/3 + 1/8 = 12/24 + 8/24 + 3/24 = 23/24. Therefore, the $500.00 that he donates to charity represents 1/24 of his total monthly paycheck. Dujuan's monthly income is $500.00 × 24, or $12,000.00. However, the question asks for the annual income, which is 12 × $12,000.00, or $144,000.00.

14. **YES:** The product of a number and its reciprocal must always equal 1. To test whether or not two numbers are reciprocals, multiply them. If the product is 1, they are reciprocals; if it is not, they are not.

$$\frac{\sqrt{3}}{2} \times \frac{2\sqrt{3}}{3} = \frac{2(\sqrt{3})^2}{2(3)} = \frac{6}{6} = 1$$

The numbers are indeed reciprocals.

15. **13:** Use Benchmark Values to estimate: 11/30 is slightly more than 1/3. 6/20 is slightly less than 1/3. Therefore, 11/30 of 6/20 of 120 should be approximately 1/3 of 1/3 of 120, or slightly more than 13. (The exact answer is 13.2.)

Chapter 3
of
FRACTIONS, DECIMALS, & PERCENTS

PERCENTS

In This Chapter . . .

- Percents as Decimals: Multiplication Shortcut
- Percents as Fractions: The Percent Table
- Benchmark Values: 10%
- Percent Increase and Decrease
- Successive Percents
- Smart Numbers: Pick 100
- Interest Formulas
- Chemical Mixtures

PERCENTS

One final way of expressing a part-whole relationship (in addition to decimals and fractions) is by using percents. Percent literally means per 100. One can conceive of percent as simply a special type of fraction or decimal that involves the number 100.

75% of the students like chocolate ice cream.

This means that, for every 100 students, 75 like chocolate ice cream.

In fraction form, we write this as $\dfrac{75}{100}$, which simplifies to $\dfrac{3}{4}$.

In decimal form, we write this as 0.75 or seventy-five hundredths. Note that the last digit of the percent is in the hundredths place value.

One common mistake is the belief that 100% equals 100. This is not correct. In fact, 100% means $\dfrac{100}{100}$, or one hundred hundredths. Therefore, 100% = 1.

Percent problems occur frequently on the GMAT. The key to these percent problems is to make them concrete by picking real numbers with which to work.

> A percent is simply a fraction with a denominator of 100.

Percents as Decimals: Multiplication Shortcut

One way of working with percents is by converting them into decimals. Percents can be converted into decimals by moving the decimal point 2 spaces to the left.

70.7% = .707	75% = .75	70% =.70 =.7	7% =.07	0.7% =.007
80.8% = .808	88% = .88	80% =.80 =.8	8% =.08	0.08% = .0008

A decimal can be converted into a percentage by moving the decimal point two spaces to the right. For example:

.6 = 60%	.28 = 28%	.459 = 45.9%	.3041 = 30.41%

Note that there are numbers greater than 100%. If 100% = 1, consider the following:

2 = 200%	3 = 300%	4.1 = 410%	5.68 = 568%

Changing percents into decimals is one way to solve "percent of" problems.

What is 65% of 500?

The phrase "percent of" (% of) signals multiplication.
> Therefore, 65% of 500 is .65(500) = 325.00 = 325.

Easy "percent of" problems can be solved in this manner—by simply changing the percentage into a decimal and then multiplying by the number in question.

Percents as Fractions: The Percent Table

Perhaps the most useful way of structuring percent problems on the GMAT is by relating percents to fractions through a percent table as shown below.

	Numbers	Percentage Fraction
PART		
WHOLE		100

This percent table can be useful for the following types of basic percent problems:

a) What is 30% of 80?
b) 75% of what number is 21?
c) 12 is what percent of 48?

In example a), we are given the whole and the percent, and we are looking for the part. Thus, we fill in the percent table as follows:

PART	x	30
WHOLE	80	100

Using the percent table, we set up a proportion, cross-multiply, and solve:

$$\frac{x}{80} = \frac{30}{100}$$

$$100x = 2,400$$
$$x = 24$$

In example b), we are given the part and the percent, and we are looking for the whole. Thus, we fill in the percent table as follows:

PART	21	75
WHOLE	x	100

Using the percent table, we set up a proportion, cross-multiply, and solve:

$$x = 28$$

In example c), we are given the part and the whole, and we are looking for the percent. Thus, we fill in the percent table as follows:

PART	12	x
WHOLE	48	100

Using the percent table, we set up a proportion, cross-multiply, and solve:

$$x = 25$$

Be careful that you have correctly identified the part and the whole when setting up your percent table.

Benchmark Values: 10%

To find 10% of any number, just move the decimal point to the left one place.

10% of 500 is 50   10% of 34.99 = 3.499   10% of .978 is .0978

You can use the Benchmark Value of 10% to estimate percents. For example:

> **Karen bought a new television, originally priced at \$690. However, she had a coupon that saved her \$67. For what percent discount was Karen's coupon?**

You know that 10% of 690 would be 69. Therefore, 67 is slightly less than 10% of 690.

Percent Increase and Decrease

Some percent problems involve the concept of percent change. For example:

> **The price of a cup of coffee increased from 80 cents to 84 cents. By what percentage did the price change?**

Percent change problems can be solved using our handy percent table. The price change (4 cents) is considered the part, while the *original* price (80 cents) is considered the whole. We are trying to solve for the percent change.

PART	4	x
WHOLE	80	100

Using the percent table, we set up a proportion, cross-multiply and solve.

$$\frac{4}{80} = \frac{x}{100}$$
$$400 = 80x$$
$$5 = x$$

Therefore, the price of a cup of coffee increased by 5%.

Alternatively, a question might be phrased as follows:

> **If a \$30 shirt decreased in price by 20%, what was the final price of the shirt?**

The whole is the original price of the shirt. The percent change is 20%. In order to find the answer, we must first find the part, which is the amount of the decrease:

PART	x	20
WHOLE	30	100

Using the percent table, we set up a proportion, cross-multiply, and solve:

$$\frac{x}{30} = \frac{20}{100}$$
$$x = 6$$

Therefore, the shirt decreased by \$6. The final price of the shirt was $30 - 6 = 24$.

The whole is the original value. It is not necessarily the largest number in the problem.

Successive Percents

One of the GMAT's favorite tricks involves successive percents.

> **If a ticket increased in price by 20%, and then increased again by 5%, by what percent did the ticket price increase in total?**

Although it may seem counter-intuitive, the answer is NOT 25%!

To understand why, consider a concrete example. Let's say that the ticket initially cost $100. After increasing by 20%, the ticket price went up to $120 ($20 is 20% of $100).

Here is where it gets tricky. The ticket price goes up again by 5%. However, it increases by 5% of the NEW PRICE of $120 (not 5% of the original $100 price). 5% of $120 is .05(120) = $6. Therefore, the final price of the ticket is $120 + $6 = $126.

You can now see that two successive percent increases, the first of 20% and the second of 5%, DO NOT result in a combined 25% increase. In fact, they result in a combined 26% increase (because the ticket price increased from $100 to $126).

Successive percents MAY NOT simply be added together! This holds for successive increases, successive decreases, and for combinations of increases and decreases (e.g. If a ticket goes up in price by 30% and then goes down by 10%, this does NOT mean that it has gone up a net of 20%).

The best way to solve successive percent problems is to choose real numbers and see what happens. The preceding example used the real value of $100 for the initial price of the ticket, making it easy to see exactly what happened to the ticket price with each increase. Usually, 100 will be the easiest real number to choose for percent problems.

Note that when you do pick numbers for successive percent problems, be sure you are very careful about which quantities each percentage refers to. Often, the different percentages will refer to different things. For example:

> **A boy eats 80% of his candy and then eats another 5% of what's left. What percentage of his original candy remains?**

Assume there are 100 pieces of candy. The boy eats 80% of them (80 pieces of candy).

Now the boy eats 5% of the *remaining* 20 pieces. (5% of 20 is 1 piece.)

Therefore, the boy has eaten 81 out of the 100 original pieces. 19% of the original candy remains.

Note that the percentages in this problem refer to different quantities. The first percentage (80%) is calculated from the original amount of candy. The second percentage (5%) is calculated from the remaining candy after the boy devours his first portion.

*Manhattan*GMAT*Prep
the new standard

Smart Numbers: Pick 100

More often than not, percent problems on the GMAT include unspecified numerical amounts; often these unspecified amounts are described by variables.

> **A shirt that initially cost _d_ dollars was on sale for 20% off. If _s_ represents the sale price of the shirt, _d_ is what percentage of _s_?**

This is an easy problem that might look confusing. To solve percent problems such as this one, simply pick 100 for the unspecified amount (just as we did when solving successive percents).

If the shirt initially cost $100, then _d_ = 100. If the shirt was on sale for 20% off, then the new price of the shirt is $80. Thus, _s_ = 80.

The question asks: _d_ is what percentage of _s_, or 100 is what percentage of 80? Using a percent table, we fill in 80 as the whole and 100 as the part (even though the part happens to be larger than the whole in this case). We are looking for the percent:

In a percent problem with unspecified amounts, pick 100 to represent the original value.

PART	100	x
WHOLE	80	100

Using the percent table, we set up a proportion, cross-multiply, and solve:

$$\frac{100}{80} = \frac{x}{100}$$
$$x = 125$$

Therefore, _d_ is 125% of _s_.

The important point here is that, like successive percent problems and other percent problems that include unspecified amounts, this example is most easily solved by plugging in a real value. For percent problems, the easiest value to plug in is 100. The fastest way to success with GMAT percent problems is to constantly pick 100!

Interest Formulas

Certain GMAT percent problems require a working knowledge of basic interest formulas. Although the compound interest formula is very rare on the GMAT, it does occasionally appear.

SIMPLE INTEREST	Principal × Rate × Time	$5,000 invested for 6 months at an annual rate of 7% will earn $175 in simple interest. Principal = $5,000, Rate = 7% or .07, Time = 6 months or .5 years. ***Prt* = $5,000(.07)(.5) = $175.00**
COMPOUND INTEREST	$P(1 + \frac{r}{n})^{nt}$, where P = principal, r = rate n = number of times per year t = number of years	$5,000 invested for 1 year at a rate of 8% compounded quarterly will earn approximately $412: $\$5{,}000\left(1 + \frac{.08}{4}\right)^{4(1)} = \$5{,}412$

Chemical Mixtures

One final type of GMAT percent problem bears mention: the chemical mixture problem.

A 500 ml solution is 20% alcohol by volume. If 100 ml of water is added, what is the new concentration of alcohol?

Chemical mixture problems can be solved systematically by using a mixture chart. Just by reading the problem, we can fill in the following for the original chemical solution:

SUBSTANCES	AMOUNT	PERCENTAGE
Alcohol		20%
Water		
TOTAL	500 ml	100%

Charts are a helpful
way to organize
information.

Before continuing, we must fill in this chart completely. If the solution is 20% alcohol, then there are .20(500) = 100 ml of alcohol. This leaves 400 ml of water, which is 80% of the solution:

SUBSTANCES	AMOUNT	PERCENTAGE
Alcohol	100 ml	20%
Water	400 ml	80%
TOTAL	500 ml	100%

Now we create a mixture chart for the altered solution. Since 100 ml of water was added, the water amount will change to 500 ml and the total amount will change to 600 ml, while the alcohol amount remains the same:

SUBSTANCES	AMOUNT	PERCENTAGE
Alcohol	100 ml	
Water	500 ml	
TOTAL	600 ml	100%

Finally, we can solve for the new alcohol percentage: $\dfrac{\text{alcohol}}{\text{total}} = \dfrac{100}{600} = .16\overline{6} = 16.\overline{6}\%$.

The key to solving these problems is creating TWO MIXTURE CHARTS—one for BEFORE (the original solution) and one for AFTER (the altered solution).

Problem Set

Solve the following problems. Use a percent table to organize percent problems, and pick 100 when dealing with unspecified amounts.

1. x% of y is 10. y% of 120 is 48. What is x?

2.   A stereo was marked down by 30% and sold for $84. What was the presale price of the stereo?

3.   From 1980-1990, the population of Kumar increased by 6%. From 1991-2000, it decreased by 3%. What was the overall percentage change in the population of Kumar from 1980-2000?

4.   If y is decreased by 20% and then increased by 60%, what is the new number, expressed in terms of y?

5.   A 7% car loan, which is compounded annually, has an interest payment of $210 after the first year. What is the principal on the loan?

6.   A bowl was half full of water. 4 cups of water were then added to the bowl, filling the bowl to 70% of its capacity. How many cups of water are now in the bowl?

7.   A large tub is filled with 920 units of alcohol and 1,800 units of water. 40% of the water evaporates. What percent of the remaining liquid is water?

8. x is 40% of y. 50% of y is 40. 16 is what percent of x?

9.   800, increased by 50% and then decreased by 30%, yields what number?

10.   Lori deposits $100 in a savings account at 2% interest, compounded annually. After 3 years, what is the balance on the account? (Assume Lori makes no withdrawals or deposits.)

11.   A full bottle contains 40% oil, 20% vinegar, and 40% water. The bottle is poured into a larger bottle, four times as big as the original. The remaining space in the larger bottle is then filled with water. If there were 8 ml of oil in the original bottle, how much water is in the final mixture?

12.   A professional gambler has won 40% of his 25 poker games for the week so far. If, all of a sudden, his luck changes and he begins winning 80% of the time, how many more games must he play to end up winning 60% of all his games for the week?

13.   If 1,600 is increased by 20%, and then reduced by y%, yielding 1,536, what is y?

14.   A certain copy machine is set to reduce an image by 13%. If Steve photocopies a document on this machine, and then photocopies the copy on the same machine, what percent of the original will his final image size be?

15.   A bottle is 80% full. The liquid in the bottle consists of 60% guava juice and 40% pineapple juice. The remainder of the bottle is then filled with 70 mL of rum. How much guava juice is in the bottle?

1. **25:** Use two percent tables to solve this problem. Begin with the fact that y% of 120 is 48:

PART	48	y
WHOLE	120	100

$$4,800 = 120y$$
$$y = 40$$

Then, set up a percent table for the fact that x% of 40 is 10.

PART	10	x
WHOLE	40	100

$$1,000 = 40x$$
$$x = 25$$

2. **$120:** Use a percent table to solve this problem. Remember that, if the stereo was marked down by 30%, the sale price represents 70% of the original price.

PART	84	70
WHOLE	x	100

$$8,400 = 70x$$
$$x = 120$$

3. **2.82% increase:** For percent problems, the Smart Number is 100. Therefore, assume that the population of Kumar in 1980 was 100. Then, apply the successive percents to find the overall percent change:

     From 1980-1990, there was a 6% increase: $100 + 100(.06) = 100 + 6 = 106$
     From 1991-2000, there was a 3% decrease: $106 - 106(.03) = 106 - 3.18 = 102.82$
     Overall, the population increased from 100 to 102.82, representing a 2.82% increase.

4. **1.28y:** For percent problems, the Smart Number is 100. Therefore, assign y a value of 100. Then, apply the successive percent to find the overall percentage change:

     (1) y is decreased by 20%: $100 - 100(.20) = 100 - 20 = 80$
     (2) Then, it is increased by 60%: $80 + 80(.60) = 80 + 48 = 128$
     Overall, there was a 28% increase. If the original value of y is 100, the new value is 1.28y.

5. **$3,000:** Use a percent table to solve this problem.

PART	210	7
WHOLE	x	100

$$21,000 = 7x$$
$$x = 3,000$$

6. **14:** There are some problems for which you cannot use Smart Numbers, since the total amount (though technically unspecified) is actually calculable. This is one of those problems. Instead, use a percent table:

PART	$.5x + 4$	70
WHOLE	x	100

$$50x + 400 = 70x$$
$$400 = 20x$$
$$x = 20$$

The capacity of the bowl is 20 cups. There are 14 cups in the bowl [70% of 20, or .5(20) + 4].

PART	4	20
WHOLE	x	100

Alternately, the 4 cups added to the bowl represent 20% of the total capacity. Use a percent table to solve for x, the whole. Since $x = 20$, there are 14 (half of 20 + 4) cups in the bowl.

7. **54%:** For this liquid mixture problem, set up a table with two columns: one for the original mixture and one for the mixture after the water evaporates from the tub.

	Original	After Evaporation
Alcohol	920	920
Water	1,800	.60(1800) = 1,080
TOTAL	2,720	2,000

The remaining liquid in the tub is $\dfrac{1,080}{2,000}$, or 54%, water.

8. **50%:** Use two percent tables to solve this problem. Begin with the fact that 50% of y is 40:

PART	40	50
WHOLE	y	100

$$4,000 = 50y$$
$$y = 80$$

Then, set up a percent table for the fact that x is 40% of y.

PART	x	40
WHOLE	80	100

$$3.200 = 100x$$
$$x = 32$$

Finally, 16 is 50% of 32.

9. **840:** Apply the successive percent to find the overall percentage change:
     (1) 800 is increased by 50%: $800 \times 1.5 = 1,200$
     (2) Then, the result is decreased by 30%: $1,200 \times .7 = 840$

10. **$106.12:** Interest compounded annually is just a series of successive percents:
     (1) 100.00 is increased by 2%: $100(1.02) = 102$
     (2) 102.00 is increased by 2%: $102(1.02) = 104.04$
     (3) 104.04 is increased by 2%: $104.04(1.02) \approx 106.12$

11. **68 mL:** First, organize the information for the original situation:
     8 mL = 40% oil x mL = 20% vinegar y mL = 40% water

There is the same amount of water in the original as there is oil. So, y = 8 mL. If you know that 8 mL is 40% of the total, then 20%, or x, must be half as much, or 4 mL. The original solution contains 20 mL of liquid all together.

	mL	%
Oil	8	40
Vinegar	4	20
Water	8	40
TOTAL	20	100

Then, the solution is poured into a new bottle with a capacity of 80 mL (4×20). The remaining space, 60 mL, is filled with water. Therefore, there are 68 mL of water in the final solution (8 from the original mixture and 60 added into the larger bottle).

	mL
Oil	8
Vinegar	4
Water	68
TOTAL	80

12. **25 more games:** Make a percent table to find out how many games the gambler has won so far.

PART	x	40
WHOLE	25	100

$1,000 = 100x$
$x = 10$
The gambler has won 10 games.

Then, make a new percent table, using a variable to represent the unknown number of additional times the gambler must play.

PART	$10 + .8n$	60
WHOLE	$25 + n$	100

$1,500 + 60n = 1,000 + 80n$
$500 = 20n$
$n = 25$
The gambler must play 25 more times.

13. **20:** Apply the percents in succession with two percent tables.

PART	x	120
WHOLE	1,600	100

$192,000 = 100x$
$x = 1,920$

Then, fill in the "change" for the part $(1920 - 1536 = 384)$ and the original for the whole (1,920).

PART	384	y
WHOLE	1,920	100

$1,920y = 38,400$
$y = 20$

14. **75.69%:** This is a series of successive percents. Use Smart Numbers to assign the original document an area of 100 square units.
    87% of 100 = .87 $\times$ 100 = 87
    87% of 87 = .87 $\times$ 87 = 75.69

15. **168 mL:** If the bottle is 80% full, then the 70 mL of rum represents the empty 20%. Use your knowledge of percents to figure out that 80% is four times as big as 20%. Therefore, there must be 4 $\times$ 70 (280) mL of the guava-pineapple mixture in the bottle. Use a percent table to find the amount of guava juice.

PART	x	60
WHOLE	280	100

$16,800 = 100x$
$x = 168$

Chapter 4
of
FRACTIONS, DECIMALS, & PERCENTS

FDP's

In This Chapter . . .

- The FDP Connection
- Converting Among Fractions, Decimals, and Percents
- Common FDP Equivalents

FDP CONNECTION

GMAT problems usually do not test fractions, decimals, and percents in isolation. Instead, most problems that test your understanding of non-integer numbers involve some kind of combination of fractions, decimals, and percents.

For this reason, we refer to these problems as FDP's (an abbreviation for fraction-decimal-percent). In order to achieve success with FDP problems on the GMAT, you must understand the connections between fractions, decimals, and percents; you should be able to comfortably and quickly shift amongst the three. In a very real sense, fractions, decimals, and percents are three different ways of expressing the exact same thing: a part-whole relationship.

> A **fraction** expresses a part-whole relationship in terms of a numerator (the part) and a denominator (the whole).

> A **decimal** expresses a part-whole relationship in terms of place value (a tenth, a hundredth, a thousandth, etc.).

> A **percent** expresses the special part-whole relationship between a number (the part) and one hundred (the whole).

> Fractions, decimals, and percents are all different ways of expressing the same thing.

Converting Among Fractions, Decimals, and Percents

The following chart reviews the ways to convert from fractions to decimals, from decimals to fractions, from fractions to percents, from percents to fractions, from decimals to percents, and from percents to decimals.

TO → FROM ↓	FRACTION $\frac{3}{8}$	DECIMAL .375	PERCENT 37.5%
FRACTION $\frac{3}{8}$		Divide the numerator by the denominator: $3 \div 8 = .375$	Divide the numerator by the denominator and move the decimal two places to the right: $3 \div 8 = .375 \rightarrow 37.5\%$
DECIMAL .375	Use the place value of the last digit in the decimal as the denominator, and put the decimal's digits in the numerator. Then simplify: $\frac{375}{1000} = \frac{3}{8}$		Move the decimal point two places to the right: $.375 \rightarrow 37.5\%$
PERCENT 37.5%	Use the digits of the percent for the numerator and 100 for the denominator. Then simplify: $\frac{37.5}{100} = \frac{3}{8}$	Find the percent's decimal point and move it two places to the left: $37.5\% \rightarrow .375$	

Common FDP Equivalents

You should memorize the following common equivalents:

Memorize these equivalents so you will recognize them quickly on the test.

Fraction	Decimal	Percent
$\frac{1}{100}$	.01	1%
$\frac{1}{50}$	.02	2%
$\frac{1}{25}$	.04	4%
$\frac{1}{20}$	.05	5%
$\frac{1}{10}$	.1	10%
$\frac{1}{8}$	.125	12.5%
$\frac{1}{6}$	$.1\overline{6}$	≈ 16.6%
$\frac{1}{5}$	.2	20%
$\frac{1}{4}$	.25	25%
$\frac{3}{10}$	.3	30%
$\frac{1}{3}$	$.\overline{3}$	≈ 33.3%
$\frac{2}{5}$	.4	40%

Fraction	Decimal	Percent
$\frac{1}{2}$	.5	50%
$\frac{3}{5}$	.6	60%
$\frac{2}{3}$	$.\overline{6}$	≈ 66.6%
$\frac{7}{10}$	.7	70%
$\frac{3}{4}$	.75	75%
$\frac{4}{5}$	.8	80%
$\frac{9}{10}$	.9	90%
$\frac{1}{1}$	1	100%
$\frac{5}{4}$	1.25	125%
$\frac{4}{3}$	$1.\overline{3}$	≈ 133%
$\frac{3}{2}$	1.5	150%

Problem Set

1. Express the following as fractions: 2.45   .008

2. Express the following as fractions: 420%   8%

3. Express the following as fractions: .15%   9.6%

4. Express the following as decimals: $\dfrac{9}{2}$ $\dfrac{3000}{10,000}$

5. Express the following as decimals: $1\dfrac{27}{3}$ $12\dfrac{8}{3}$

6. Express the following as decimals: 2,000%   .030%

7. Express the following as percents: $\dfrac{1000}{10}$ $\dfrac{25}{9}$

8. Express the following as percents: 80.4   .0007

9. Express the following as percents: 36.1456   1

10. Order from least to greatest: $\dfrac{8}{18}$ .8   40%

11. Order from least to greatest: 1.19 $\dfrac{120}{84}$ 131.44%

12. Order from least to greatest: $2\dfrac{4}{7}$ 2400%   2.401

13. Order from least to greatest ($x \neq 0$): $\dfrac{50}{17}x^2$ $2.9x^2$ $(x^2)(3.10\%)$

14. Order from least to greatest: $\dfrac{500}{199}$ 248,000%   2.9002003

15. Order from least to greatest: $\dfrac{3}{5}$ $\dfrac{.00751}{.01}$ $\dfrac{200}{3} \times 10^{-2}$

    $\dfrac{8}{10}$

1. To convert a decimal to a fraction, write it over the appropriate power of ten and simplify.

$$2.45 = 2\frac{45}{100} = 2\,\frac{9}{20}$$

$$.008 = \frac{8}{1000} = \frac{1}{125}$$

2. To convert a percent to a fraction, write it over a denominator of 100 and simplify.

$$420\% = \frac{420}{100} = \frac{21}{5} = 4\frac{1}{5}$$

$$8\% = \frac{8}{100} = \frac{2}{25}$$

3. To convert a percent that contains a decimal to a fraction, write it over a denominator of 100. Shift the decimal points in the numerator and denominator to eliminate the decimal point in the numerator. Then simplify.

$$.15\% = \frac{.15}{100} = \frac{15}{10000} = \frac{3}{2000}$$

$$9.6\% = \frac{9.6}{100} = \frac{96}{1000} = \frac{12}{125}$$

4. To convert a fraction to a decimal, divide the numerator by the denominator.

$$\frac{9}{2} = 9 \div 2 = 4.5$$

It often helps to simplify the fraction BEFORE you divide:

$$\frac{3000}{10,000} = \frac{3}{10} = .3$$

5. To convert a mixed number to a decimal, simplify the mixed number first, if needed.

$$1\frac{27}{3} = 1 + 9 = 10$$

$$12\frac{8}{3} = 12 + 2\frac{2}{3} = 14\frac{2}{3} = 14.\overline{6}$$

6. To convert a percent to a decimal, drop the percent sign and shift the decimal point two places to the left.

$$2{,}000\% = 20$$
$$.030\% = .00030$$

7. To convert a fraction to a percent, rewrite the fraction with a denominator of 100.

$$\frac{1000}{10} = \frac{10000}{100} = \textbf{10,000\%}$$

Or convert the fraction to a decimal and shift the decimal point two places to the right.

$$\frac{25}{9} = 25 \div 9 = 2.\overline{7} = \textbf{277.}\overline{\textbf{7}}\textbf{\%}$$

8. To convert a decimal to a percent, shift the decimal point two places to the right.

$80.4 = \textbf{8040\%}$

$.0007 = \textbf{.07\%}$

9. To convert a decimal to a percent, shift the decimal point two places to the right.

$36.1456 = \textbf{3614.56\%}$

$1 = \textbf{100\%}$

10. **40% < 8/18 < .8:** To order from least to greatest, express all the terms in the same form.

$8/18 = .\overline{4}$

$.8 = .8$

$40\% = .4$

$.4 < .\overline{4} < .8$

Alternately, you can use FDP logic and Benchmark Values to solve this problem: 8/18 is 1/18 less than 1/2. 40% is 10% (or 1/10) less than 1/2. Since 8/18 is a smaller piece away from 1/2, it is closer to 1/2 and therefore larger than 40%. .8 is clearly greater than 1/2. Therefore, 40% < 8/18 < .8.

11. **1.19 < 131.44% < 120/84:** To order from least to greatest, express all the terms in the same form.

$1.19 = 1.19$

$120/84 \approx 1.4286$

$131.44\% = 1.3144$

$1.19 < 1.3144 < 1.4286$

12. **2.401 < 2 4/7 < 2400%:** To order from least to greatest, express all the terms in the same form.

$$2\frac{4}{7} \approx 2.57$$

$2400\% = 24$

$2.401 = 2.401$

Alternately, you can use FDP logic and Benchmark Values to solve this problem: 2400% is 24, which is clearly the largest value. Then, use Benchmark Values to compare 2 4/7 and 2.401. Since the whole number portion, 2, is the same, just compare the fraction parts. 4/7 is greater than 1/2. .401 is less than 1/2. Therefore, 2 4/7 must be greater than 2.401. So, 2.401 < 2 4/7 < 2400%.

13. **3.10% < 2.9 < 50/17:** To order from least to greatest, express all the terms in the same form. (Note that, since x^2 is a positive term common to all the terms you are comparing, you can ignore its presence completely.)

$$\frac{50}{17} = 2\frac{16}{17} \approx 2.94$$

2.9 = 2.9
3.10% = .0310
.0310 < 2.9 < 2.94

Alternately, you can use FDP logic and Benchmark Values to solve this problem: 3.10% is .0310, which is clearly the smallest value. Then, compare 2.9 and 2 16/17 to see which one is closer to 3. 2.9 is 1/10 away from 3. 2 16/17 is 1/17 away from 3. Since 1/17 is a smaller piece than 1/10, 2 16/17 is closest to 3; therefore, it is larger. So, 3.10% < 2.9 < 50/17.

14. **500/199 < 2.9002003 < 248,000%:** To order from least to greatest, express all the terms in the same form.

$$\frac{500}{199} \approx 2.51$$

248,000% = 2,480
2.9002003 = 2.9002003

Alternately, you can use FDP logic and Benchmark Values to solve this problem: 248,000% = 2,480, which is clearly the largest value. 500/199 is approximately 500/200, or 5/2, which is 2.5. This is clearly less than 2.9002003. Therefore, 500/199 < 2.9002003 < 248,000%.

15. $\dfrac{200}{3} \times 10^{-2} < \dfrac{3}{5} \div \dfrac{8}{10} < \dfrac{.0751}{.01}$

First, simplify all terms and express them in decimal form:

$$\frac{3}{5} \div \frac{8}{10} = \frac{3}{5} \times \frac{10}{8} = \frac{3}{4} = .75$$

$$\frac{.00751}{.01} = \frac{.751}{1} = .751$$

$$\frac{200}{3} \times 10^{-2} = 66.\overline{6} \times 10^{-2} = .\overline{6}$$

$$.\overline{6} < .75 < .751$$

Chapter 5
of
FRACTIONS, DECIMALS, & PERCENTS

STRATEGIES FOR
DATA SUFFICIENCY

In This Chapter . . .

- Rephrasing: One Equation, One Variable
- Sample Rephrasings for Challenging Problems

Rephrasing: One Equation, One Variable

Data sufficiency problems that deal with FDP's usually present various parts and wholes. Keeping track of them can be difficult. Therefore, one strategy to help you solve these problems is to REPHRASE questions and statements into equations in order to keep track of what you know and what you need to know. Your ultimate goal in writing equations is to combine them in such a way that you are left with a single equation with only one variable. The variable in the equation should represent the quantity you are asked to find in the original question.

If a brokerage firm charged a commission of 2% of the total dollar amount of a certain trade, what was the total dollar amount of that trade?

(1) The dollar amount of the trade minus the brokerage firm's commission was $88,000.
(2) The brokerage firm's commission decreased the profit earned on the trade by 20%.

Try to rephrase the part-whole relationship given in the question by writing an equation.

A   Statement (1) ALONE is sufficient, but statement (2) alone is not sufficient.
B   Statement (2) ALONE is sufficient, but statement (1) alone is not sufficient.
C   BOTH statements TOGETHER are sufficient, but NEITHER statement ALONE is sufficient.
D   EACH statement ALONE is sufficient.
E   Statements (1) and (2) together are NOT sufficient.

First, assign a variable to represent the unknown for which you are trying to solve:

Let d = the total dollar amount of the trade

Then, express the information given in the question, identifying any other variables you need:

Let c = the brokerage firm's commission

$c = .02d$

Test each statement, writing equations to represent the information. If the information in the statement can be combined with the information in the question to yield a single equation with the single variable d, the statement is sufficient:

Statement (1): $d - c = 88,000$

Substitute the value for c given in the question.

$d - (.02d) = 88,000$

This is a single equation with a single variable so it is sufficient to solve for d and answer the question.

DATA SUFFICIENCY STRATEGY

Statement (2) introduces a new variable into the picture: profit.

Let p = the profit before the commission

$p - c = 0.80p$

Since we do not know p, the amount of profit from the trade before the commission, we cannot solve for c, the brokerage firm's commission.

Since we cannot find c, we are unable to determine d, the total dollar amount of the trade. Thus, statement (2) is NOT sufficient.

The answer to this data sufficiency problem is (A): Statement (1) ALONE is sufficient, but statement (2) alone is not sufficient.

Beware of statements that introduce too many variables. These are usually not sufficient to answer the question.

Rephrasing: Challenge Short Set

At the very end of this book, you will find lists of FRACTIONS, DECIMALS, & PERCENTS problems that have appeared on past official GMAT exams. These lists reference problems from *The Official Guide for GMAT Review, 11th Edition* and *The Official Guide for GMAT Quantitative Review* (the questions contained therein are the property of The Graduate Management Admission Council, which is not affiliated in any way with Manhattan GMAT).

As you work through the Data Sufficiency problems listed at the end of this book, be sure to focus on *rephrasing*. If possible, try to *rephrase* each question into its simplest form *before* looking at the two statements. In order to rephrase, focus on figuring out the specific information that is absolutely necessary to answer the question. After rephrasing the question, you should also try to *rephrase* each of the two statements, if possible. Rephrase each statement by simplifying the given information into its most basic form.

In order to help you practice rephrasing, we have taken the most difficult Data Sufficiency problems on *The Official Guide* problem list (these are the problem numbers listed in the "Challenge Short Set" on page 81) and have provided you with our own sample rephrasings for each question and statement. In order to evaluate how effectively you are using the rephrasing strategy, you can compare your rephrased questions and statements to our own rephrasings that appear below. Questions and statements that are significantly rephrased appear in **bold**.

Rephrasings from *The Official Guide For GMAT Review, 11th Edition*

The questions and statements that appear below are only our *rephrasings*. The original questions and statements can be found by referencing the problem numbers below in the Data Sufficiency section of *The Official Guide for GMAT Review, 11th edition* (pages 278-290).

55.   Let d = the number of guests served a double scoop
        Let s = the number of guests served a single scoop

    What is the value of d?

    (1) **$.6(d + s) = d$**

    (2) **$2d + s = 120$**

110.   Let t = the tens digit of the bill
        Let u = the units digit of the bill
        $10t + u$ = the amount of the bill
        $2t$ = the amount of the tip

    Is $2t > .15(10t + u)$?
    Is $2t > 1.5t + .15u$?

    Is $\dfrac{10t}{3} > u$?

    (1) **$1 \le t \le 4$**

    (2) **$2t = 8$**
        $t = 4$

111.   Let x = the original price of stock X
        Let y = the original price of stock Y

        What is the value of $\dfrac{.9y}{x}$?

What is the value of $\dfrac{y}{x}$?

(1) $1.1x = y$

$$\dfrac{y}{x} = 1.1$$

(2) $.1x = (\dfrac{10}{11}).1y$

$$\dfrac{y}{x} = \dfrac{11}{10}$$

150.   Let a = the regular price of the most expensive item
        Let b = the regular price of the second most expensive item
        Let c = the regular price of the least expensive item

        Is $.2a + .1b + .1c > .15(a + b + c)$?
                Is $.05a > .05b + .05c$?

Is $a > b + c$?

(1) $a = 50, \ b = 20, \ c < 20$

(2) $c = 15, \ b > 15, \ a > 15$

Rephrasings from *The Official Guide for* GMAT *Quantitative Review*

The questions and statements that appear below are only our *rephrasings*. The original questions and statements can be found by referencing the problem numbers below in the Data Sufficiency section of *The Official Guide for GMAT Quantitative Review* (pages 149-157).

5. Let x = the percent discount at which the TV was bought
    Let y = the percent mark-up at which the TV was sold
    Let z = the original (list) price

    Purchase Price = $z \times \dfrac{(100 - x)}{100}$ and Sale Price = $z \times \dfrac{(100 - y)}{100}$

    What is the value of z?

    (1) $x = 15$

    (2) $y = x - 5$

22. Let s = money awarded to the spouse
    Let a = money awarded to the oldest child
    Let b = money awarded to the middle child
    Let c = money awarded to the youngest child
    $s + a + b + c = 200,000$
    $c = 200,000 - (a + b + s)$

    What is the value of c?

    (1) $s = 100,000$
        $a = 25,000$

    (2) $b = c$
        $a = c - 12,500$
        $s = c + 62,500$

48. The easiest way to solve this problem is to test numbers, making sure to test both integer and decimal values for r and s.

49.   Let n = the number of shares

What is the value of $\dfrac{12{,}000}{n}$?

What is the value of n?

(1) $n(\dfrac{12{,}000}{n} + 1) = \$12{,}300$

$\quad\quad 12000 + n = \$12{,}300$
$\quad\quad\quad\quad\quad\quad\quad\quad n = 300$

(2) $n(\dfrac{12{,}000}{n} - 2) = .95(\$12{,}300)$

$\quad\quad 12{,}000 - 2n = 11{,}400$
$\quad\quad\quad\quad\quad 2n = 600$
$\quad\quad\quad\quad\quad\quad n = 300$

72.   Let r = the number of games remaining for Team A
Let t = total number of games played by Team A = $20 + r$
Let w = games won by Team A = $10 + r$

What is the value of w?
Better: What is the value of r?

(1) $t = 25$
(2) $\dfrac{w}{t} = \dfrac{10 + r}{20 + r} = .60$

$\quad\quad 10 + r = 12 + .6r$
$\quad\quad\quad .4r = 2$
$\quad\quad\quad\quad r = 5$

113.   The easiest way to solve this problem is to test numbers.

Chapter 6
of
FRACTIONS, DECIMALS, & PERCENTS

OFFICIAL GUIDE
PROBLEM SETS

In This Chapter . . .

- Fractions, Decimals, & Percents Problem Solving List from *The Official Guides*
- Fractions, Decimals, & Percents Data Sufficiency List from *The Official Guides*

Practicing with REAL GMAT Problems

Now that you have completed your study of FRACTIONS, DECIMALS, & PERCENTS, it is time to test your skills on problems that have actually appeared on real GMAT exams over the past several years.

The problem sets that follow are composed of questions from two books published by the Graduate Management Admission Council® (the organization that develops the official GMAT exam):

The Official Guide for GMAT Review, 11th Edition &
The Official Guide for GMAT Quantitative Review

These two books contain quantitative questions that have appeared on past official GMAT exams. (The questions contained therein are the property of The Graduate Management Admission Council, which is not affiliated in any way with Manhattan GMAT.)

Although the questions in the Official Guides have been "retired" (they will not appear on future official GMAT exams), they are great practice questions.

In order to help you practice effectively, we have categorized every problem in The Official Guides by topic and subtopic. On the following pages, you will find two categorized lists:

(1) **Problem Solving:** Lists all Problem Solving FRACTION, DECIMAL, & PERCENT questions contained in *The Official Guides* and categorizes them by subtopic.

(2) **Data Sufficiency:** Lists all Data Sufficiency FRACTION, DECIMAL, & PERCENT questions contained in *The Official Guides* and categorizes them by subtopic.

Note: Each book in Manhattan GMAT's 8-book preparation series contains its own *Official Guide* lists that pertain to the specific topic of that particular book. If you complete all the practice problems contained on the *Official Guide* lists in the back of each of the 8 Manhattan GMAT preparation books, you will have completed every single question published in *The Official Guides*. At that point, you should be ready to take your Official GMAT exam!

Problem Solving

from *The Official Guide for GMAT Review, 11th edition* (pages 20-23 & 152-186) and *The Official Guide for GMAT Quantitative Review* (pages 62-85)

<u>Note</u>: Problem numbers preceded by "D" refer to questions in the Diagnostic Test chapter of *The Official Guide for GMAT Review, 11th edition* (pages 20-23).

Solve each of the following problems in a notebook, making sure to demonstrate how you arrived at each answer by showing all of your work and computations. If you get stuck on a problem, look back at the FDP strategies and content in this guide to assist you.

CHALLENGE SHORT SET

This set contains the more difficult FDP problems from each of the content areas.

> *11th edition*: D11, D12, 115, 138, 142, 156, 165, 175, 177, 228, 237, 240
> *Quantitative Review*: 33, 37, 41, 73, 79, 100, 101, 120, 134, 142, 143, 159, 165, 167

FULL PROBLEM SET

Fractions

> *11th edition*: D8, 14, 40, 42, 77, 84, 96, 109, 117, 138, 162, 174, 175, 183, 188, 198, 221, 243
> *Quantitative Review*: 5, 11, 37, 39, 44, 46, 48, 51, 57, 61, 73, 79, 88, 108, 112, 134, 135, 154, 162, 165, 167, 176

Digits and Decimals

> *11th edition*: D1, D11, 12, 66, 113, 129, 133, 143, 184, 194, 219, 228, 244
> *Quantitative Review*: 2, 4, 41, 65, 66, 93, 142, 174

Percents

> *11th edition*: D21, 6, 17, 34, 44, 48, 59, 75, 78, 100, 104, 123, 128, 131, 139, 156, 165, 197, 240
> *Quantitative Review*: 8, 10, 13, 24, 33, 47, 74, 95, 101, 114, 120, 138, 143, 156, 158, 159

Successive Percents and Percent Change

> *11th edition*: D12, 15, 62, 80, 94, 110, 115, 151, 177, 237
> *Quantitative Review*: 6, 36, 40, 67, 89, 100

FDP's

> *11th edition*: 8, 22, 53, 83, 142, 189
> *Quantitative Review*: 25, 27, 43, 56

Data Sufficiency

from *The Official Guide for GMAT Review, 11th edition* (pages 24-25 & 278-290) and *The Official Guide for GMAT Quantitative Review* (pages 149-157)

Note: Problem numbers preceded by "D" refer to questions in the Diagnostic Test chapter of *The Official Guide for GMAT Review, 11th edition* (pages 24-25).

Solve each of the following problems in a notebook, making sure to demonstrate how you arrived at each answer by showing all of your work and computations. If you get stuck on a problem, look back at the FDP strategies and content contained in this guide to assist you.

Practice REPHRASING both the questions and the statements by using variables and constructing equations. The majority of data sufficiency problems can be rephrased; however, if you have difficulty rephrasing a problem, try testing numbers to solve it.

It is especially important that you familiarize yourself with the directions for data sufficiency problems, and that you memorize the 5 fixed answer choices that accompany all data sufficiency problems.

CHALLENGE SHORT SET
This set contains the more difficult FDP problems from each of the content areas.
>*11th edition*: 55, 110, 111, 150
>*Quantitative Review*: 5, 22, 48, 49, 72, 113

FULL PROBLEM SET
Fractions
>*11th edition*: 31, 84,
>*Quantitative Review*: 2, 22, 113

Digits and Decimals
>*11th edition*: D25, 16, 35, 45, 58
>*Quantitative Review*: 30, 44, 48

Percents
>*11th edition*: D40, 1, 7, 55, 59, 74, 77, 150
>*Quantitative Review*: 5, 36, 49, 52, 72, 89

Successive Percents and Percent Change
>*11th edition*: 91
>*Quantitative Review*: 1

FDP's
>*11th edition*: 4, 8, 34, 46, 62, 69, 107, 110, 111

To waive "Finance I" at Harvard Business School you must:
    (A) Be a CFA
    (B) Have prior coursework in finance
    (C) Have two years of relevant work experience in the financial sector
    (D) Pass a waiver exam
    (E) None of the above; one cannot waive core courses at HBS

What are the requirements of an Entrepreneurial Management major at the Wharton School?
    (1) Completion of 5 credit units (cu) that qualify for the major
    (2) Participation in the Wharton Business Plan Competition during the 2nd year of the MBA program
(A) Statement (1) ALONE is sufficient, but statement (2) alone is not sufficient.
(B) Statement (2) ALONE is sufficient, but statement (1) alone is not sufficient.
(C) BOTH statements TOGETHER are sufficient, but NEITHER statement ALONE is sufficient.
(D) EACH statement ALONE is sufficient.
(E) Statements (1) and (2) TOGETHER are NOT sufficient.

Once You Ace the GMAT, Get Ready to Ace Your Applications!

To make an informed decision in applying to a school—and to craft an effective application that demonstrates an appreciation of a program's unique merits—**it's crucial that you do your homework.** Clear Admit School Guides cut through the gloss of marketing materials to give you the hard facts about a program, and then put these school-specific details in context so you can see how programs compare. In the guides, you'll find detailed, comparative information on vital topics such as:

- The core curriculum and first-year experience
- Leading professors in key fields
- Student clubs and conferences
- Full-time job placement by industry and location
- Student demographics
- International and experiential learning programs
- Tuition, financial aid and scholarships
- Admissions deadlines and procedures

Now available for top schools including:
Chicago, Columbia, Harvard, Kellogg, MIT, Stanford, Tuck and Wharton

A time-saving source of comprehensive information, Clear Admit School Guides have been featured in *The Economist* and lauded by applicants, business school students and MBA graduates:

"Purchasing the Clear Admit HBS School **Guide was one of best decisions I made.** I visited HBS three times and have every book and pamphlet that covers the top business schools, but nothing can compare to the Clear Admit guides in offering up-to-date information on every aspect of the school's academic and social life that is not readily available on the school's website and brochures. Reading a Clear Admit School Guide gives an applicant the necessary, detailed school information to be competitive in the application process."
—An applicant to Harvard

CLEAR ADMIT
School Guides

"I want to tip my hat to the team at Clear Admit that put these guides together. I'm a recent graduate of Wharton's MBA program and remain active in the admissions process (serving as an alumni interviewer to evaluate applicants). I can't tell you how important it is for applicants to show genuine enthusiasm for Wharton and I think the Clear Admit School Guide for Wharton captures many of the important details, as well as the spirit of the school. **This sort of information is a must for the serious MBA applicant.**"
—A Wharton MBA graduate

Question #1: (e) and Question #2 (a)

www.clearadmit.com/schoolguides

contact us at mbaguides@clearadmit.com

Finally, a GMAT* prep guide series that goes beyond the basics.

Reading Comprehension, 2007 Edition
ISBN: 978-0-9790175-6-8
Retail: $26

Critical Reasoning, 2007 Edition
ISBN: 978-0-9790175-5-1
Retail: $26

Word Translations, 2007 Edition
ISBN: 978-0-9790175-3-7
Retail: $26

Number Properties, 2007 Edition
ISBN: 978-0-9790175-0-6
Retail: $26

Geometry, 2007 Edition
ISBN: 978-0-9790175-4-4
Retail: $26

Equations, Inequalities, & VIC's, 2007 Edition
ISBN: 978-0-9790175-2-0
Retail: $26

Sentence Correction, 2007 Edition
ISBN: 978-0-9790175-7-5
Retail: $26

Fractions, Decimals, & Percents, 2007 Edition
ISBN: 978-0-9790175-1-3
Retail: $26

Published by

Manhattan **GMAT** *Prep*

☑ You get many more pages per topic than found in all-in-one tomes.

☑ Only buy those guides that address the specific skills you need to develop.

☑ Gain access to Online Practice GMAT* Exams & bonus question banks.

COMMENTS FROM GMAT TEST TAKERS:

Now Available at your local bookstore!

"Bravo, Manhattan GMAT! Bravo! The guides truly did not disappoint. All the guides are clear, concise, and well organized and explained things in a manner that made it possible to understand things the first time through without missing any of the important details."

"I've thumbed through a lot of books that don't even touch these. The fact that they're split up into components is immeasurably helpful. The set-up of each guide and the lists of past GMAT problems make for an incredibly thorough and easy to follow study path."